A Challenging Peace
in the Life and Stories of Jesus

D1598615

A Challenging Peace

in the Life and Stories of Jesus

Art and Reflections by
Cara B. Hochhalter

Epigraph Books
Rhinebeck, New York

Book design by Colin Rolfe

ISBN 978-1-948796-82-8

Library of Congress Control Number 2019909740

Epigraph Books
22 East Market Street, Suite 304
Rhinebeck, New York 12572
(845) 876-4861
epigraphps.com

This book is dedicated to my family, Jeff and Anna, and to all of us worldwide who believe that a more peace-filled world is possible.

Contents

Introduction		1
1. Mary Visits Elizabeth	Luke 1:39-55	4
2. The Nativity	Luke 2:4-20	6
3. The Magi	Matthew 2:1-12	8
4. The Baptism of Jesus	Luke 3:21-22	10
5. Three Temptations	Luke 4:1-13	12
6. Water into Wine	John 2:1-11	14
7. Reading from the Torah	Luke 4:14-20	16
8. From the Lord's Prayer	Luke 11:1-4	18
9. Transfiguration	Luke 9:28-36	20
10. Blessed are those...but woe...	Luke 6:17-26	22
11. Let Your Light Shine	Matthew 5:14-16	24
12. Consider the Lilies	Matthew 6:25-29, 33	26
13. Woman at the Well	John 4:5-15	28
14. Woman with the Alabaster Jar	Luke 7:36-50	30
15. Calming the Storm	Mark 4:35-41	32
16. Just a Touch	Mark 5:24b-34	34
17. Martha and Mary	Luke 10:38-42	36
18. Feeding the Multitudes	Matthew 14:13-21	38
19. Even the Dogs	Mark 7:24-30	40

20.	Welcoming the Children	Mark 10:13-16	42
21.	Zacchaeus	Luke 19:1-10	44
22.	A Parable: The Good Samaritan	Luke 10:29-37	46
23.	A Parable: Where to Sit?	Luke 14:1,7-14	48
24.	A Parable: The Lost Sheep	Luke 15:1-7	50
25.	A Parable: The Lost Coin	Luke 15: 8-10	52
26.	A Parable: The Mustard Seed	Luke 13:18-19	54
27.	A Parable: The Sower	Luke 8:4-8	56
28.	A Parable: The Prodigal Leaves	Luke 15:11-13a	58
29.	The Prodigal Turns	Luke 15:13b-19	60
30.	The Prodigal is Welcomed	Luke 15:20-21	62
31.	The Celebration	Luke 15:22-24	64
32.	The Elder Brother	Luke 15:25-32	66
33.	As a Hen Gathers	Luke 13:31-34	68
34.	Palm Sunday: Even the Stones	Luke 19:28-40	70
35.	Maundy Thursday Foot-Washing	John 13:1-17	72
36.	Communion/Eucharist	Mark 14:22-25	74
37.	When They Crucified Jesus	John 19:23-31a,38-42	76
38.	Easter Morning	Luke 24:1-9	80
39.	On the Road to Emmaus	Luke 24:13-35	82
40.	Swords into Plowshares	Isaiah 2:2-4	86
Notes			88
Acknowledgments			90
About the Author			92

Introduction

Jesus was ultimately a peacemaker. His life and stories are a challenge *to* us and a challenge *for* us to live in this way. The stories engage us to seek an individual relationship with God in our unique ways of understanding God, and to hold an inclusive love for others. It is a challenge to draw from this faith to put principles of truth-telling, love, compassion and forgiveness into action to promote peace.

Jesus never advocated revenge or violent retribution in the face of conflict. He never rallied armies to protect him because he knew that violence only begets violence. Rather, Jesus made peace through the power of an Infinite Love; a love that he knew from his relationship in and with God. It is a way of loving others and even one's enemies, through creative compassion.

Over the last thirty years, through my work as a Christian Educator, a student at United Theological Seminary of the Twin Cities, and then as an ordained UCC minister recently retired, I have been creating images that interpret these powerful stories around the life of Jesus. The stories are beautiful, challenging, poignant, and relevant for our lives and times. I believe these stories hold universal truths not limited to Christianity.

There are three parts to each of the interpretations of these forty stories. First is the visual image. After meditation and study of the biblical texts, the images were created through the process of block-printing. Each block was carved so that what would be dark was raised in relief and the white areas were removed so that the ink did not remain there. Ink was rolled over the block and paper was placed on top. A spoon was used to press the paper against the block and then pulled off carefully. The print always looks backwards from what was carved on the block, which is a little surprising. But after all, Jesus' stories were often a reversal of what people expected.

The interaction of light and dark is important in each image. One cannot have one without the other because the light *defines* the dark, and vice versa. I find this to be theological as we look to the whole—the light *and* the dark, the joy *and* the despair, the peace *and* the conflict—all under an umbrella of Divine Love that yearns for wholeness.

As an individual or a small group, you might begin by looking at the image first. What do you see there? Are there parts of it that make you wonder or question? Do you see humor in it? What do you remember about the story that it interprets? Does it remind you of something in your own life?

The second interpretation is the scripture text itself, taken from the *New Revised Standard Version of The Holy Bible*. You might read it in a fresh way by paying attention to the visual descriptions. What do you *see* in the story? Is this depicted in the block-print? Are there parts of the scripture that you have not imagined before? Does the art offer new ideas about the story? How do the text and the art affirm the idea of Jesus as peacemaker? Do you feel yourself being challenged in some ways?

The third interpretation is my reflection on both the text and the image. I share how new insights become relevant through the process of creating each block print. The images themselves become interpretations rather than illustrations and the texts take on new meaning through the art. The images and questions also give you, the viewer, the opportunity to explore these stories from your own experiences and to discover your own interpretations. The life and stories of Jesus challenge us all towards making peace in our hearts, in our communities and in our world. In the mystery of God's Creative Spirit, may these stories come alive to engage us all into a future of fulfilled peace.

1. Mary Visits Elizabeth

Luke 1:39-55

In those days Mary set out and went with haste to a Judean town in the hill country, where she entered the house of Zechariah and greeted Elizabeth. When Elizabeth heard Mary's greeting, the child leaped in her womb. And Elizabeth, filled with the Holy Spirit exclaimed with a loud cry, "Blessed are you among women, and blessed is the fruit of your womb. And why has this happened to me, that the mother of my Lord comes to me? For as soon as I heard the sound of your greeting, the child in my womb leaped for joy. And blessed is she who believed that there would be a fulfillment of what was spoken to her by the Lord."

And Mary said, "My soul magnifies the Lord, and my spirit rejoices in God my Savior, for he has looked with favor on the lowliness of his servant.

Surely, from now on all generations will call me blessed; for the Mighty One has done great things for me, and holy is his name. God's mercy is for those who fear him from generation to generation and has shown strength with his arm; he has scattered the proud in the thoughts of their hearts. He has brought down the powerful from their thrones, and lifted up the lowly; God has filled the hungry with good things, and sent the rich away empty.

He has helped the servant Israel, in remembrance of God's mercy, according to the promise he made to our ancestors, to Abraham and to his descendants forever."

✝

What an intimate scene between Mary and her cousin. They are both with child and Elizabeth's baby seems to recognize the child within Mary's womb! In my image, the cat even looks pregnant as the whole scene vibrates with joy and expectation.

In a celebration of new life and promise, Mary rather unexpectedly repeats a song from the Hebrew scriptures of justice for the poor and the ending of economic disparity. Looking back, the Gospel-writers suggested that, even before Jesus was born, there was hope that he would usher in a way of peacemaking. Jesus would hold God's vision for peace through his very being, the way he lived his life, and in the stories he told.

My focus through these visual interpretations of scripture and reflections is the challenging peace that Jesus longed for us to understand. It is a way towards peace that continues to call us in our own times.

2. The Nativity

Luke 2:4-20

Joseph also went from the town of Nazareth in Galilee to Judea, to the city of David called Bethlehem, because he was descended from the house and family of David. He went to be registered with Mary, to whom he was engaged and who was expecting a child. While they were there, the time came for her to deliver her child. And she gave birth to her firstborn son and wrapped him in bands of cloth, and laid him in a manger, because there was no place for them in the inn.

In that region there were shepherds living in the fields, keeping watch over their flock by night. Then an angel of the Lord stood before them, and the glory of the Lord shone around them, and they were terrified. But the angel said to them, "Do not be afraid; for see—I am bringing you good news of great joy for all the people: to you is born this day in the city of David a Savior, who is the Messiah, the Lord. This will be a sign for you: you will find a child wrapped in bands of cloth and lying in a manger." And suddenly there was with the angel a multitude of the heavenly host, praising God and saying, "Glory to God in the highest heaven, and on earth peace among those whom he favors!"

When the angels had left them and gone into heaven, the shepherds said to one another, "Let us go now to Bethlehem and see this thing that has taken place, which the Lord has made known to us." So they went with haste and found Mary and Joseph, and the child lying in the manger. When they saw this, they made known what had been told them about this child; and all who heard it were amazed at what the shepherds told them. But Mary treasured all these words and pondered them in her heart. The shepherds returned, glorifying and praising God for all they had heard and seen, as it had been told them.

It is a humble story of Jesus' birth. He was not born out of wealth and riches. This story teaches all of us, and particularly children who act out the nativity every Christmas, that wealth does not matter. Jesus, who held God in his very being, came into the world as a person on the margins, a refugee whose family could find no home of their own and were later sent into exile. But that did not matter either.

In this image, Jesus is surrounded by love; from Mary and Joseph, from animals—and soon shepherds would come. It is a story about how an infinite love can rise up from any place and move us all forward with a yearning for peace among all creation.

3. The Magi

Matthew 2:1-12

In the time of King Herod, after Jesus was born in Bethlehem of
Judea, wise men from the East came to Jerusalem, asking, "Where is
the child who has been born king of the Jews? For we observed his star
at its rising, and have come to pay him homage." When King Herod
heard this, he was frightened, and all Jerusalem with him; and calling
together all the chief priests and scribes of the people, he inquired of
them where the Messiah was to be born. They told him, "In Bethlehem
of Judea; for so it has been written by the prophet:

'And you, Bethlehem, in the land of Judah, are by no means least among the rulers of Judah; for from you shall come a ruler who is to shepherd my people Israel.'"

Then Herod secretly called for the wise men and learned from them the exact time when the star had appeared. Then he sent them to Bethlehem, saying, "Go and search diligently for the child; and when you have found him, bring me word so that I may also go and pay him homage."

When they had heard the king, they set out; and there, ahead of them, went the star that they had seen at its rising, until it stopped over the place where the child was. When they saw that the star had stopped, they were overwhelmed with joy. On entering the house, they saw the child with Mary his mother; and they knelt down and paid him homage. Then, opening their treasure chests, they offered him gifts of gold, frankincense, and myrrh. And having been warned in a dream not to return to Herod, they left for their own country by another road.

It is told that Magi, astrologers from other surrounding nations, also came to see this child. This story implies that, although Jesus was of humble background, those who were wealthy, educated, and from faraway places were also lured to this child of peace.

I included a woman riding a camel in this image, for certainly there were also women who studied the stars and looked for signs—rich and poor, people of all races and backgrounds responded to the love that Jesus would teach. It is a love meant to cross all cultural boundaries, even today.

Perhaps if we could see the possibilities and hope in every new birth, in every new beginning, and in every humble start; we might also find there— the peace of God.

4. The Baptism of Jesus *Luke 3:21-22*

Now when all the people were baptized, and when Jesus also had been baptized and was praying, the heaven was opened, and the Holy Spirit descended upon him in bodily form like a dove. And a voice came from heaven, "You are my Son, the Beloved; with you I am well pleased."

Jesus was baptized in the Jordan River amid the beauty of creation, not at a baptismal font inside a temple. He experienced the spirit and peace of God fall upon him as the heavens opened up. Imagine God's Spirit falling upon him "like a dove."

I created this image while staying in a cabin in the Cascade Mountains of Washington State. The window looked out on the Skykomish River—and I imagined Jesus being baptized there.

In the incredible beauty of our natural world, perhaps we all have had that sense of holiness falling upon us. For me, it comes with a feeling of connection and love in the midst of natural beauty. It is a blessing that invites me to live in ways that promote peace for this earth and all its inhabitants.

In the process of creating this print, I turned the block, making a shadow image. How surprising to see another face appear on Jesus' chest! Suddenly the words from scripture became clear. "And a voice came from heaven, 'You are my Son, the Beloved…'"

Jesus would hold God within him—and show us all how we might also carry God, and be carried by God, throughout our lives.

5. Three Temptations

Luke 4:1-13

Jesus, full of the Holy Spirit, returned from the Jordan and was led by the Spirit in the wilderness, where for forty days he was tempted by the devil. He ate nothing at all during those days, and when they were over, he was famished. The devil said to him, "If you are the Son of God, command this stone to become a loaf of bread." Jesus answered him, "It is written, 'One does not live by bread alone.'"

Then the devil led him up and showed him in an instant all the kingdoms of the world. And the devil said to him, "To you I will give their glory and all this authority; for it has been given over to me, and I give it to anyone I please. If you, then, will worship me, it will all be yours."

Jesus answered him, "It is written, 'Worship the Lord your God, and serve only him.'"

Then the devil took him to Jerusalem, and placed him on the pinnacle of the temple, saying to him, "If you are the Son of God, throw yourself down from here, for it is written, 'He will command his angels concerning you, to protect you,' and 'On their hands they will bear you up, so that you will not dash your foot against a stone.'"

Jesus answered him, "It is said, 'Do not put the Lord your God to the test.'" When the devil had finished every test, he departed from him until an opportune time.

It seemed the perfect place to create this image while on retreat at The Monastery of Christ in the Desert, near Abiquiu, New Mexico. The three temptations are depicted as the devil challenges Jesus to turn stone into bread, to become a ruler over all, and to test the angels' protection. My image of Jesus did not look as anguished as I imagined when faced with temptations that would lure him away from his being in God.

With a separate block depicting the Cholla cactus that grew along the paths in New Mexico, I created an overlay print. Someone told me, "Now it looks 'prickly'!" What a good description of those times when we are tempted to use our own power and gifts for selfish reasons.

If we can hold our focus on God, however we understand this inner source of Divine Truth, then we need not test the limits of Infinite Love.

6. Water into Wine

John 2:1-11

On the third day there was a wedding in Cana of Galilee, and the mother of Jesus was there. Jesus and his disciples had also been invited to the wedding. When the wine gave out, the mother of Jesus said to him, "They have no wine."

And Jesus said to her, "Woman, what concern is that to you and to me? My hour has not yet come."

His mother said to the servants, "Do whatever he tells you."

Now standing there were six stone water jars for the Jewish rites of purification, each holding twenty or thirty gallons.

Jesus said to them, "Fill the jars with water." And they filled them up to the brim.

He said to them, "Now draw some out, and take it to the chief steward."

So they took it. When the steward tasted the water that had become wine, and did not know where it came from (though the servants who had drawn the water knew), the steward called the bridegroom and said to him, "Everyone serves the good wine first, and then the inferior wine after the guests have become drunk. But you have kept the good wine until now."

Jesus did this, the first of his signs, in Cana of Galilee, and revealed his glory; and his disciples believed in him.

The Gospel of John is the only one that tells of this miracle at the beginning of Jesus' ministry. Jesus and his mother are at a wedding, and the wine runs out. This is humiliating for the family, and Mary asks Jesus to do something. He says he is not really ready for this but Mary tells the servants to go ahead and do whatever Jesus asks. So the servants pour water into the large earthen vessels, and out comes excellent wine.

Jesus often exaggerated to make a point. In my image, the size of the vessels was accentuated. Perhaps the largeness of these earthen vessels points to the abundance of generosity that Jesus presented when someone was in a situation of shame or humiliation.

Although, perhaps it was Mary's sense of justice (and hospitality) that really is at work in this story!

7. **Reading from the Torah** *Luke 4:14-20*

Then Jesus, filled with the power of the Spirit, returned to Galilee, and a report about him spread through all the surrounding country. He began to teach in their synagogues and was praised by everyone.

When he came to Nazareth, where he had been brought up, he went to the synagogue on the Sabbath day, as was his custom. He stood up to read, and the scroll of the prophet Isaiah was given to him. He unrolled the scroll and found the place where it was written:

"The Spirit of the Lord is upon me,
because he has anointed me
to bring good news to the poor.
He has sent me to proclaim release to the captives
and recovery of sight to the blind,
to let the oppressed go free,
to proclaim the year of the Lord's favor."

And he rolled up the scroll, gave it back to the attendant, and sat down. The eyes of all in the synagogue were fixed on him. Then he began to say to them, "Today this scripture has been fulfilled in your hearing." All spoke well of him and were amazed at the gracious words that came from his mouth. They said, "Is not this Joseph's son?"

When Jesus reads from scripture in the temple, his choice of texts is important. "Filled with the power of the Spirit," he reads from the words of Isaiah describing the idea of Jubilee; good news for the poor, release to those in captivity, healing for the sick, and freedom for all people oppressed. It is a reminder of the Magnificat, the song that Mary sang before Jesus was even born.

Amazingly, Jesus followed his reading by saying that in their hearing of these words today, the scripture was fulfilled. In their hearing of the words, something was taking place! Did he mean that henceforth, they would be inspired to proclaim justice and peace for all? Was it to remind them that even a son of their own community could hold the Spirit of God and aspire to bring justice—just as they also would do? I think these words of scripture are still longing to be fulfilled, in our own hearing.

In my image of the Torah, there are bumps and curves, shadows and light, yet the hope for God's Jubilee is there to be discovered.

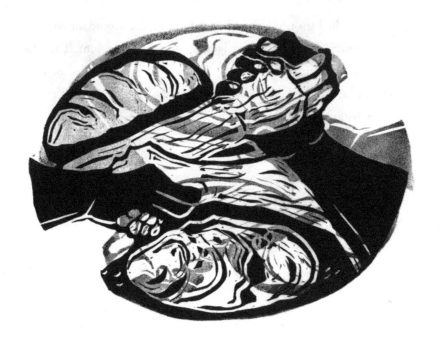

8. From the Lord's Prayer   *Luke 11:1-4*

He was praying in a certain place, and after he had finished, one of his disciples said to him, "Lord, teach us to pray, as John taught his disciples." He said to them, "When you pray, say:

> Father[Creator], hallowed be your name.
> Your kingdom come.
> Give us each day our daily bread.
> And forgive us our sins,
> for we ourselves forgive everyone indebted to us.
> And do not bring us to the time of trial."

We hear the "Lord's Prayer" a little differently in this version from Luke. I focused on feeding and forgiving, these two aspects of the prayer Jesus taught. Being hungry and being in debt make people poor in our country and world. Then, so often people become victims of their own poverty.

In my image there are two loaves of bread and the whole image is also in the shape of bread. Jesus implies that our food comes from God's great ecology. How do we show our gratitude? What is our responsibility as consumers in a system of food production and distribution? Are the ways that we are fed helpful or hurtful for the world's hungry?

The hands in the image are clasped in demonstration of reconciliation and forgiveness. Perhaps God's kingdom (kin-dom) comes on earth as we focus on feeding and forgiving, on bread and friendship, and finding equitable solutions for those who are in debt.

I turned the block upside-down for a secondary printing which adds complexity and dimension to the image. Peace is not a simple process. It may seem like a tangle of issues and politics, yet Jesus affirms that feeding and forgiving play a large part in moving us towards peace for all.

9. Transfiguration

Luke 9:28-36

Now about eight days after these sayings Jesus took with him Peter and John and James, and went up on the mountain to pray. And while he was praying, the appearance of his face changed, and his clothes became dazzling white. Suddenly they saw two men, Moses and

Elijah, talking to him. They appeared in glory and were speaking of his departure, which he was about to accomplish at Jerusalem.

Now Peter and his companions were weighed down with sleep; but since they had stayed awake, they saw his glory and the two men who stood with him. Just as they were leaving him, Peter said to Jesus, "Master, it is good for us to be here; let us make three dwellings, one for you, one for Moses, and one for Elijah"—not knowing what he said. While he was saying this, a cloud came and overshadowed them; and they were terrified as they entered the cloud.

Then from the cloud came a voice that said, "This is my Son, my Chosen; listen to him!" When the voice had spoken, Jesus was found alone. And they kept silent and in those days told no one any of the things they had seen.

‡

It is out of a time of retreat into prayer with three of his disciples that suddenly Jesus appears to be elevated spiritually. There is a whirl of energy in this image and story. Jesus is seen shimmering with Divine Light. Alongside him appear great prophets of the faith from the past, Moses (with tablets) and Elijah (by a broom tree).

In the story, the disciples were astounded beyond words. In their thrill of the moment, they want to build a shrine, a memorial to mark this incredible occurrence.

But God seems to have another answer. They are covered by a cloud and out of it God speaks, telling them to listen to what Jesus says; that he has been chosen by God. Perhaps it is more important that the disciples really hear what Jesus has to say than to idolize and worship him in that place. Questions might be raised about our own tendency to create idols that may or may not help us listen to the Divine.

10. Blessed are those...but woe...

Luke 6:17-26

He came down with them and stood on a level place, with a great crowd of his disciples and a great multitude of people from all Judea, Jerusalem, and the coast of Tyre and Sidon. They had come to hear him and to be healed of their diseases; and those who were troubled with unclean spirits were cured. And all in the crowd were trying to touch him, for power came out from him and healed all of them. Then he looked up at his disciples and said:

"Blessed are you who are poor, for yours is the kingdom of God.

"Blessed are you who are hungry now, for you will be filled.
"Blessed are you who weep now, for you will laugh.

"Blessed are you when people hate you, and when they exclude you, revile you, and defame you on account of the Son of Man. Rejoice in that day and leap for joy, for surely your reward is great in heaven; for that is what their ancestors did to the prophets.

"But woe to you who are rich, for you have received your consolation.
"Woe to you who are full now, for you will be hungry.
"Woe to you who are laughing now, for you will mourn and weep.

"Woe to you when all speak well of you, for that is what their ancestors did to the false prophets."

This is a sobering version of the Beatitudes as read in the Gospel of Luke. While the poor are blessed, Jesus goes on to chastise those who are wealthy at the expense of the poor!

I was thinking of the farm workers in Florida who pick tomatoes. The Coalition of Immokalee Workers, who after many years of demonstrations have gotten companies to sign on to their national campaign called The Fair Food Program. It is an award-winning human rights initiative that has helped to raise wages and eliminate abuses.

This image begs for the conversation about our own "riches." Are they attained at the expense of others? How does the image make you feel? What issues does it bring up? Might Jesus cry out for a system in which all are dignified by their labors, with living wages and equitable working conditions?

11. Let Your Light Shine   *Matthew 5:14-16*

"You are the light of the world. A city built on a hill cannot be hid. No one after lighting a lamp puts it under the bushel basket, but on the lampstand, and it gives light to all in the house. In the same way, let your light shine before others, so that they may see your good works and give glory to God in heaven."

While Jesus urged his disciples to be humble, in this text he encourages them not to hide their light. If the infinite life-giving light of God is in all creation, including us, then it may seem paradoxical to let this light shine even as we seek humility. Perhaps we might let God's light be reflected in the ways we live and act in this world, knowing that it comes from a source within but also beyond ourselves—and no matter what our religion, we do not have an exclusive right to this spiritual essence of being.

It is a challenge to see this light of Holiness everywhere, even in those with whom we have difficulty; to see the light of Love even in our enemies. The life and stories of Jesus are a demonstration of this way of nonviolence and loving across the divisions.

The interplay of light and dark is crucial in the carving of the blocks for these prints. I am constantly thinking about what is going to be light and what is going to be dark; for one informs and defines the other. The radiating rays of light in this image would mean nothing without the surrounding dark. Perhaps this way of looking leads to a non-duality that sees the wholeness of God's realm in all life.

In the image, I turned the block upside down to create a "shadow" print. Once again, I was surprised at what appeared. There is an echo of the flame, in reverse, in the candle itself. It is an inner light that is exactly what Jesus tells us not to hide. Perhaps finding this light inspires our own good works in the world, as we also look for it in others.

12. Consider the Lilies   *Matthew 6:25-29, 33*

"Therefore I tell you, do not worry about your life, what you will eat or what you will drink, or about your body, what you will wear. Is not life more than food, and the body more than clothing?

Look at the birds of the air; they neither sow nor reap nor gather into barns, and yet God feeds them. Are you not of more value than they?

And can any of you by worrying add a single hour to your span of life? And why do you worry about clothing? Consider the lilies of the field, how they grow; they neither toil nor spin, yet I tell you, even Solomon in all his glory was not clothed like one of these..."

"...But strive first for the kingdom of God and his righteousness, and all these things will be given to you as well."

Yes, let us consider the lilies of the field and the birds of the air! In this beautiful text, Jesus reminds us to place ourselves within the context of our natural world. Are we not also part of this miraculous eco-system where all are cared for when there is balance? Jesus asks why we would worry about what we wear and what we will eat when we are part of this environment of abundance and beauty.

Jesus says it is more important that we strive to be right with God, and our material needs will fall into place. In our age of consumerism, however, it seems that we do need to be concerned with how what we wear and what we eat affects the well-being of our natural world and other people.

If Jesus saw how we are putting our earth in peril, he might have told us to consider our environment with much more concern and urgency. To be right with God means to care about the ways in which our human actions affect the future of this miraculous creation.

In my image, the flower is one that grows in the Holy Land and covers the fields in a blue color. The shape of the image reminds me of a thumb print—perhaps God's thumbprint on our Earth! I like the movement that asks us to examine our human footprint on our environment.

13. Woman at the Well

John 4:5-15

So he came to a Samaritan city called Sychar, near the plot of ground that Jacob had given to his son Joseph. Jacob's well was there, and Jesus, tired out by his journey, was sitting by the well. It was about noon.

A Samaritan woman came to draw water, and Jesus said to her, "Give me a drink." (His disciples had gone to the city to buy food.) The Samaritan woman said to him, "How is it that you, a Jew, ask a drink of me, a woman of Samaria?" (Jews do not share things in common with Samaritans.) Jesus answered her, "If you knew the gift of God, and who it is that is saying to you, 'Give me a drink,' you would have asked him and he would have given you living water."

The woman said to him, "Sir, you have no bucket, and the well is deep. Where do you get that living water? Are you greater than our ancestor Jacob, who gave us the well, and with his sons and his flocks drank from it?"

Jesus said to her, "Everyone who drinks of this water will be thirsty again, but those who drink of the water that I will give them will never be thirsty. The water that I will give will become in them a spring of water gushing up to eternal life."

The woman said to him, "Sir, give me this water, so that I may never be thirsty or have to keep coming here to draw water."

In many of the stories, Jesus, as peacemaker, reaches across societal boundaries to show God's inclusive love for all people. In this story, he crosses two boundaries. One is people of a different religious practice (Samaritans were Jewish but had an age-old difference of opinion about where they could worship. This disagreement led to animosity to such an extent that they were not to even speak to one another.) The other boundary he crosses is speaking to a woman.

Jesus talks to her about living water—the infinite love of an eternal God—that has filled him and could fill her also. She, perhaps playfully, takes a literal meaning and asks how he could reach this deep water without a bucket!

The story goes on to reveal that Jesus knows about her past life with many husbands but demonstrates his forgiveness. This is part of the living water of God's infinite love: to cross boundaries and to offer a profound forgiveness with the expectation of reconciliation and healing.

14. Woman with the Alabaster Jar

Luke 7:36-50

One of the Pharisees asked Jesus to eat with him, and he went into the Pharisee's house and took his place at the table. And a woman in the city, who was a sinner, having learned that he was eating in the Pharisee's house, brought an alabaster jar of ointment. She stood behind him at his feet, weeping, and began to bathe his feet with her tears and to dry them with her hair. Then she continued kissing his feet and anointing them with the ointment.

Now when the Pharisee who had invited him saw it, he said to himself, "If this man were a prophet, he would have known who and what kind of woman this is who is touching him—that she is a sinner." Jesus spoke up and said to him, "Simon, I have something to say to you." "Teacher," he replied, "speak."

"A certain creditor had two debtors; one owed five hundred denarii, and the other fifty. When they could not pay, he canceled the debts for both of them. Now which of them will love him more?" Simon answered, "I suppose the one for whom he canceled the greater debt." And Jesus said to him, "You have judged rightly."

Then turning toward the woman, he said to Simon, "Do you see this woman? I entered your house; you gave me no water for my feet, but she has bathed my feet with her tears and dried them with her hair. You gave me no kiss, but from the time I came in she has not stopped kissing my feet. You did not anoint my head with oil, but she has anointed my feet with ointment.

Therefore, I tell you, her sins, which were many, have been forgiven; hence she has shown great love. But the one to whom little is forgiven, loves little." Then he said to her, "Your sins are forgiven." But those who were at the table with him began to say among themselves, "Who is this who even forgives sins?" And he said to the woman, "Your faith has saved you; go in peace."

What a story of the power of forgiveness. In the house of one of the Pharisees, who were religious leaders of the day, a woman who is considered a "sinner" comes in to anoint the feet of Jesus and wipe them with her hair. Jesus is criticized for allowing her to touch him. Jesus tells a story about debtors who are forgiven and which of these would be the most grateful—the one forgiven most or the one forgiven least? This woman is forgiven much and so she loves greatly in gratitude and humility. Once again Jesus crosses societal boundaries to express the infinite love and forgiveness of God for all people.

The Pharisees wonder who Jesus thinks he is by forgiving sins, but Jesus tells the woman that it was her faith that saved her—that she may go in peace. Don't we all know that sense of peace that follows forgiveness?

In my image, Jesus has a halo, or nimbus, but the woman also is embraced by light. Notice the size of the two figures.

15. Calming the Storm

Mark 4:35-41

On that day, when evening had come, he said to them, "Let us go across to the other side." And leaving the crowd behind, they took him with them in the boat, just as he was. Other boats were with him.

A great windstorm arose, and the waves beat into the boat, so that the boat was already being swamped. But he was in the stern, asleep on the cushion; and they woke him up and said to him, "Teacher, do you not care that we are perishing?"

He woke up and rebuked the wind, and said to the sea, "Peace! Be still!" Then the wind ceased, and there was a dead calm. He said to them, "Why are you afraid? Have you still no faith?"

And they were filled with great awe and said to one another, "Who then is this, that even the wind and the sea obey him?"

✝

Jews and Gentiles lived "on the other side" of the Sea of Galilee. It seems that Jesus did not want to confine his teachings to just a small community. He crossed over to reach beyond his own circle of followers.

While the disciples take him with them in the boat, a mighty storm comes up. Jesus does not sit passively by, even though his disciples have to wake him up (sometimes we need others to alert us), then he actively confronts the trouble. He commands the disturbances to be still. He takes the initiative and becomes an active peacemaker. His followers are amazed that even the wind and sea obey him.

Jesus asks them about their own fears. Are they so filled with fear that they cannot see the possibilities for peace in any given situation? Is their fear keeping them from confronting difficulties? This is a story of hope, for as Jesus had God at his center, he dared to command peace in the face of crisis. And we might do the same.

I was fortunate to travel with a group who were visiting peacemakers in Israel and Palestine. When we were on a boat on the Sea of Galilee, the sun was shining brightly when a dramatic storm suddenly came upon us. The waves rolled and sheets of rain poured down. It was over in a matter of minutes, and the sea returned to calm once again. This story came alive for me as I literally experienced a "calming of the storm." Perhaps peace can come just as instantly.

16. **Just a Touch**

Mark 5:24b-34

And a large crowd followed him and pressed in on him. Now there was a woman who had been suffering from hemorrhages for twelve years. She had endured much under many physicians, and had spent all that she had; and she was no better, but rather grew worse.

She had heard about Jesus, and came up behind him in the crowd and touched his cloak, for she said, "If I but touch his clothes, I will be made well." Immediately her hemorrhage stopped; and she felt in her body that she was healed of her disease.

Immediately aware that power had gone forth from him, Jesus turned about in the crowd and said, "Who touched my clothes?"

And his disciples said to him, "You see the crowd pressing in on you; how can you say, 'Who touched me?'"

He looked all around to see who had done it. But the woman, knowing what had happened to her, came in fear and trembling, fell down before him, and told him the whole truth. He said to her, "Daughter, your faith has made you well; go in peace, and be healed of your disease."

This story demonstrates the tangibility of God's healing power. The woman was convinced that if she could only touch the fringe of Jesus' cloak, she might be healed. Amazingly, Jesus feels this interaction of touch and healing, even as the crowd pushes in on him.

When I was a teenager, my mother was diagnosed with a cancer that led her to explore her faith in terms of God's healing light and love. I saw how her meditation and prayers had real effects on her spiritual and physical well-being. "Touching" an infinite healing power through prayer may very well accompany and enhance the healing efforts of doctors, medicines, and surgery.

One time, when I had minor surgery I held a little piece of paper in my hand with a prayer written on it. It was by Christina Rossetti; "Open wide the window of my spirit and fill me full of light." Before the anesthesia, I asked the doctor what I should do with my piece of paper. He said, "How about if I put it in my shirt pocket?" It was a beautiful, tangible act that affirmed a place for prayer in healing.

On the last day of my mother's life, she told me that she could "feel my prayers." In the mystery of faith and healing love, somehow our prayers become tangible. Think about times you have "touched holiness"—through individual meditation and prayer, communal worship, serving others, contemplating the beauty of nature, working for peace, or other ways.

17. Martha and Mary   *Luke 10:38-42*

N ow as they went on their way, he entered a certain village, where a woman named Martha welcomed him into her home. She had a sister named Mary, who sat at the Lord's feet and listened to what he was saying.

But Martha was distracted by her many tasks; so she came to him and asked, "Lord, do you not care that my sister has left me to do all the work by myself? Tell her then to help me." But Jesus answered her,

"Martha, Martha, you are worried and distracted by many things; there is need of only one thing. Mary has chosen the better part, which will not be taken away from her."

A friend of mine, who loves to cook, complained that Martha gets a bad rap in this story when she should be honored for making the meal! So I focused on Martha. I wanted to capture her exasperation of feeling torn between her obligation to provide a meal and wanting to hear what stories Jesus was telling her sister. Many of us who prepare meals can relate to this situation.

We also might relate to Martha when she gets a little perturbed. Why isn't her sister helping her? Perhaps Martha is jealous and a little childishly angry as she asks Jesus to make Mary help. The stories around Jesus touch on very human feelings that we can see in ourselves today.

Perhaps Jesus was reminding us to let go of so many distractions and details, to let go of sibling rivalry and jealousies, and to realize the importance of finding spiritual balance in our lives. However, I welcome and am grateful for the opportunity to cook and serve and for those who share hospitality in this way.

Perhaps there is a way to meet both our contemplative needs and our desire for doing at the same time. I am reminded of the seventeenth-century lay monk, Brother Lawrence, who spent years learning how to "practice the presence of God" at the same time that he was doing ordinary chores such as preparing meals for the monastery. What a delightful challenge for us.

18. Feeding the Multitudes   *Matthew 14:13-21*

N ow when Jesus heard this, he withdrew from there in a boat to a deserted place by himself. But when the crowds heard it, they followed him on foot from the towns. When he went ashore, he saw a great crowd; and he had compassion for them and cured their sick.

When it was evening, the disciples came to him and said, "This is a deserted place, and the hour is now late; send the crowds away so that they may go into the villages and buy food for themselves."

Jesus said to them, "They need not go away; you give them something to eat."

They replied, "We have nothing here but five loaves and two fish."

And Jesus said, "Bring them here to me." Then he ordered the crowds to sit down on the grass. Taking the five loaves and the two fish, he looked up to heaven, and blessed and broke the loaves, and gave them to the disciples, and the disciples gave them to the crowds.

And all ate and were filled; and they took up what was left over of the broken pieces, twelve baskets full. And those who ate were about five thousand men, besides women and chilldren.

Jesus has just heard about the death of John the Baptist and he seeks a deserted place to be by himself, but the crowds follow him. He has compassion for them and heals their sick.

This story is told in all four gospels giving it significance. It describes a situation to which we can all relate. It is late, people are hungry and there is seemingly not enough food. The disciples want to send the crowd away to buy food in the villages, but Jesus says something that seems impossible. He tells them to feed the people themselves.

In this metaphorical miracle, Jesus takes the five loaves and two fish, he blesses them—giving thanks to God, breaks the bread, and then gives them to the disciples to feed the people. After all are fed, there are twelve baskets of broken pieces left.

The act of giving thanks to God for whatever we have is key to this story. This act of gratitude and invitation for God to enter into the situation places the focus beyond our own limitations.

It is not Jesus who feeds the people in this miraculous way, but the disciples in the love of God. In my image, one disciple has his hand out ready to participate in this way of abundant giving—and one disciple is turned away in doubt.

It is heartbreaking to think of the amount of hunger in the world when we are told that there is enough. We see so much waste. Perhaps it is about recognizing the miracle of sharing and our own abilities to help others—focusing on abundance and not scarcity.

Do you see the twelve baskets? Do you suppose the disciples took these home with the left-overs?

19. Even the Dogs   *Mark 7:24-30*

From there he set out and went away to the region of Tyre. He entered a house and did not want anyone to know he was there. Yet he could not escape notice, but a woman whose little daughter had an unclean spirit immediately heard about him, and she came and bowed down at his feet.

Now the woman was a Gentile, of Syrophoenician origin. She begged him to cast the demon out of her daughter. He said to her, "Let the children be fed first, for it is not fair to take the children's food and throw it to the dogs."

But she answered him, "Sir, even the dogs under the table eat the children's crumbs."

Then he said to her, "For saying that you may go—the demon has left your daughter." So she went home, found the child lying on the bed, and the demon gone.

✝

This story is often referred to as a time when even Jesus made a mistake and changed his mind. It is also a time when he listens to someone he perceives as "less than" and learns. How important this is in the process of peacemaking.

Once again, Jesus tries to find some quiet time, but a Gentile (a Syrophoenician woman) finds him there. She bows at his feet and asks that her child be healed.

Presumably, Jesus is talking about his own people as the children of God whom he says deserve to be fed first, and not have their food fed to the dogs. What an insulting thing to say and so uncharacteristic of our perception of Jesus. It is a wonder the writers of both Matthew and Mark include this story, but the fact that it is included, gives us reason to ponder it.

The woman is quick and responds cleverly, "Even the dogs under the table eat the children's crumbs." All people deserve to have their basic needs met; to have access to food and healthcare.

Perhaps Jesus is impressed by her boldness or her telling truth to power. In the Matthew version, Jesus says it is her faith that is to be commended. Whatever the reason, Jesus changes his mind and sends her home to find her daughter healed.

I am imagining Jesus responding to the Me Too; Black Lives Matter; and Poor People's Campaign movements of today and saying, "Yes, you also matter and deserve justice and fairness."

20. Welcoming the Children *Mark 10:13-16*

People were bringing little children to him in order that he might touch them; and the disciples spoke sternly to them.

But when Jesus saw this, he was indignant and said to them, "Let the little children come to me; do not stop them; for it is to such as these that the kingdom of God belongs. Truly I tell you, whoever does not receive the kingdom of God as a little child will never enter it."

And he took them up in his arms, laid his hands on them and blessed them.

This wonderful story affirms the value of children. In spite of objections from the disciples, Jesus says to let the children come to him.

Not only should children be welcomed, blessed, and loved, but Jesus says that we might look to children regarding how to know God's realm of peace in this world. Not all children are the same, but within a sense of innocence there can also be compassion, truth-telling, and a desire for what is fair for people and animals.

Perhaps Jesus was also suggesting that we embrace God with a sense of childlike curiosity and wonder. How might we embrace more openness, with hopeful expectation for goodness in our world as demonstrated by Jesus—and children?

21. Zacchaeus

Luke 19:1-10

He entered Jericho and was passing through it. A man was there named Zacchaeus; he was a chief tax collector and was rich. He was trying to see who Jesus was, but on account of the crowd he could not, because he was short in stature. So he ran ahead and climbed a sycamore tree to see him, because he was going to pass that way.

When Jesus came to the place, he looked up and said to him, "Zacchaeus, hurry and come down; for I must stay at your house today." So he hurried down and was happy to welcome him. All who saw it began to grumble and said, "He has gone to be the guest of one who is a sinner."

Zacchaeus stood there and said to the Lord, "Look, half of my possessions, Lord, I will give to the poor; and if I have defrauded anyone of anything, I will pay back four times as much." Then Jesus said to him, "Today salvation has come to this house, because he too is a son of Abraham. For the Son of Man came to seek out and to save the lost."

What a turn-around! The forgiveness and dignity that Jesus bestows on this tax collector, who has become wealthy by taking advantage of others, allows Zacchaeus to turn his life around and make amends in a generous way.

As I look at the image, it seems as though I am in the tree with Zacchaeus. I am the one looking over the crowd towards Jesus and I may be the one who is surprised by an invitation for forgiveness. Could it be that the Christ of Universal Love always desires to come into our homes and share bread with us? Again, Jesus reaches across boundaries to demonstrate peacemaking through God's inclusive love.

22. A Parable: The Good Samaritan

Luke 10:29-37

But wanting to justify himself, he [a lawyer] asked Jesus, "And who is my neighbor?"

Jesus replied, "A man was going down from Jerusalem to Jericho, and fell into the hands of robbers, who stripped him, beat him, and went away, leaving him half dead. Now by chance a priest was going down that road; and when he saw him, he passed by on the other side. So likewise a Levite, when he came to the place and saw him, passed by on the other side.

But a Samaritan while traveling came near him; and when he saw him, he was moved with pity. He went to him and bandaged his wounds, having poured oil and wine on them. Then he put him on his own animal, brought him to an inn, and took care of him. The next day he took out two denarii, gave them to the innkeeper, and said, 'Take care of him; and when I come back, I will repay you whatever more you spend.'

Which of these three, do you think, was a neighbor to the man who fell into the hands of the robbers?" He said, "The one who showed him mercy."

Jesus said to him, "Go and do likewise."

The title of this parable points to its poignancy because Samaritans were not seen as "good" in the eyes of the Jews around Jesus. They were considered "outsiders," and it would have been a jolt to the hearers of the story that the Samaritan was the one who offered help.

Once again, Jesus teaches not only crossing boundaries to offer love, friendship, and understanding, but to see our adversaries as human beings who are worthy of good deeds! It is the way towards peace between races, nationalities, and people of differing faiths, political views, and sexual orientations. Looking beyond differences to demonstrate compassion is a powerful story that Jesus knew would bring us closer to the peace of God.

In my image, the road could also be seen as a kind of river that flows with compassion and mercy.

23. A Parable: Where to Sit? *Luke 14:1,7-14*

On one occasion when Jesus was going to the house of a leader of the Pharisees to eat a meal on the Sabbath, they were watching him closely....

When he noticed how the guests chose the places of honor, he told them a parable. "When you are invited by someone to a wedding banquet, do not sit down at the place of honor, in case someone more distinguished than you has been invited by your host; and the host who invited both of you may come and say to you, 'Give this person your place,' and then in disgrace you would start to take the lowest place. But when you are invited, go and sit down at the lowest place, so that when your host comes, he may say to you, 'Friend, move up higher'; then you will be honored in the presence of all who sit at the table with you. For all who exalt themselves will be humbled, and those who humble themselves will be exalted."

He said also to the one who had invited him, "When you give a luncheon or a dinner, do not invite your friends or your brothers or your relatives or rich neighbors, in case they may invite you in return, and you would be repaid. But when you give a banquet, invite the poor, the crippled, the lame, and the blind. And you will be blessed, because they cannot repay you, for you will be repaid at the resurrection of the righteous."

It was a custom in Jesus' time to sit on cushions when having a meal (although, in my image they look more like beanbags). It was also important where people sat; those of more prestige sitting in a place of honor in the center.

Jesus suggests that one should not assume the place of honor at a banquet because he or she might be embarrassed if asked to move. Rather, he suggests a more humble position to begin with, and then it might be pleasant to be asked to move up.

This parable pushes us to examine our own egos when interacting in the world. Do we subconsciously assume that we are "better than" others? Are we okay with taking a more humble attitude? This kind of humility does not mean we let others take advantage of us but that we can be confident in seeing ourselves as part of a larger whole. It may seem ironic when Jesus says the more humble we see ourselves, the higher we are lifted up in God's eyes!

Almost as an afterthought, Jesus suggests that if we are going to have a dinner party, it would be better to invite outcasts rather than those from whom we seek approval just to make us "look good."

In our efforts to make peace in this world, we might stand with the hungry, the war-weary, and the poor. We might join with others working for peace out of a sense of humility and not to receive attention or praise. Perhaps Jesus knew that it is freeing—to release the need to be the center of attention.

24. A Parable: The Lost Sheep   *Luke 15:1-7*

Now all the tax collectors and sinners were coming near to listen to him. And the Pharisees and the scribes were grumbling and saying, "This fellow welcomes sinners and eats with them."

So he told them this parable: "Which one of you, having a hundred sheep and losing one of them, does not leave the ninety-nine in the wilderness and go after the one that is lost until he finds it? When he has found it, he lays it on his shoulders and rejoices. And when he comes home, he calls together his friends and neighbors, saying to them,

'Rejoice with me, for I have found my sheep that was lost.' Just so, I tell you, there will be more joy in heaven over one sinner who repents than over ninety-nine righteous persons who need no repentance.

This parable and the next one call our attention to the very human situation of losing something and then finding it. We all know the joy of that experience. In this image, even the heavens seem to be rejoicing as a little shepherd finally finds his lost lamb.

Jesus suggests that the glory of reconciling in relationship with God is multiplied many times over—and no one is left behind.

25. A Parable: The Lost Coin   *Luke 15:8-10*

"Or what woman having ten silver coins, if she loses one of them, does not light a lamp, sweep the house, and search carefully until she finds it? When she has found it, she calls together her friends and neighbors, saying, 'Rejoice with me, for I have found the coin that I had lost.' Just so, I tell you, there is joy in the presence of the angels of God over one sinner who repents."

In this story, Jesus tells of a woman who has lost one of her ten coins. She sweeps the house thoroughly and rejoices when she finds it. We all know that feeling of finally finding something, whether it is a book, a note, or perhaps a feeling of faith. Jesus seems to be saying that, in God's expansive love that yearns to be found for each one of us, there is such joy when the connection is made or rediscovered. This "finding" of an Infinite and Holy Love may happen at any time, even in each moment.

In both of these parables, there is so much rejoicing over the found thing that the neighbors and friends are called in to celebrate. Don't we all rather excitedly tell someone when something precious is found? Perhaps this is a key part of these lost and found parables: that as we find glimpses of God/Holiness/Divine Love, there is a desire to share.

26. A Parable: The Mustard Seed

Luke 13:18-19

He said therefore, "What is the kingdom of God like? And to what should I compare it? It is like a mustard seed that someone took and sowed in the garden; it grew and became a tree, and the birds of the air made nests in its branches."

The kingdom (or "kin-dom") of God, the realm of God, God's vision for justice and peace—is profuse. Jesus surprises his hearers by using a mustard seed as a metaphor. Everyone knew that mustard was invasive and one would never plant it in a garden.

Perhaps Jesus is telling them that a tiny packet of God's yearning for peace has the potential to grow like a tree and even upset an order of oppression!

If we nurture its growth, Jesus says that birds from many nations will long to come and build nests in its branches. For something even as small as a seed of love, can have transforming power and create an environment where others long to reside.

While this parable has been used to teach how a small bit of faith can grow within one's individual life, the parable may also be about how a small bit of Holy Love can transform our relations in our larger society, our world, and with our Earth.

27. A Parable: The Sower

Luke 8:4-8

When a great crowd gathered and people from town after town came to him, he said in a parable: "A sower went out to sow his seed; and as he sowed, some fell on the path and was trampled on, and the birds of the air ate it up. Some fell on the rock; and as it grew up, it withered for lack of moisture. Some fell among thorns, and the thorns grew with it and choked it. Some fell into good soil, and when it grew, it produced a hundredfold." As he said this, he called out, "Let anyone with ears to hear listen!"

✝

Who is the sower in this parable that Jesus told? Is it God, Jesus, or perhaps our own hands reaching out to share a life-giving love with others? The parable points to obstacles that interfere with this "Word" being heard.

What are the barriers that keep us from hearing? Is there something holding us back from allowing a Divine Love to take hold in our own lives? Even if we hear a plea for peacemaking in the great ecology of all creation, are we hesitant to take action? What would be empowering?

Rather unintentionally, the shape of my image looks like a loaf of bread. Bread (or rice in many parts of the world) gives life. However, Jesus said, "It is written, 'One does not live by bread alone, but by every word that comes from the mouth of God.'" (Mt 4:4.) Perhaps we can find ways to take within the soil of our own beings, the wisdom and word of God's love and peace.

It may be through prayer and meditation that we become more receptive. Being part of faith communities can also inspire our openness and strengthen our actions as we join with others to make peace.

I am inspired by the many people, of all faiths, who live out this "Way" through generous acts of sharing, compassion, and selflessness for the good of others. They may be small ways like caring for plants and sharing food, or large ways of working for justice in larger systems. A multitude of opportunities surround us, yet perhaps it takes some intentionality to see around the obstacles that hold us back.

28. A Parable: The Prodigal Leaves

Luke 15:11-13a

Then Jesus said, "There was a man who had two sons. The younger of them said to his father, 'Father, give me the share of the property that will belong to me.' So he divided his property between them. A few days later the younger son gathered all he had and traveled to a distant country...."

These five images are all scenes from the incredible parable of a wayward son returning home, well-known as "The Prodigal Son." It is another of the "lost and found" parables.

In this first scene, we see the son who has asked for his inheritance (early) and is taking off. This would have shocked the hearers of the story as it was customary for the elder son, not the younger, to receive the inheritance and not until after the father had died.

For the poor forlorn parents I included the mother, who seems to be trying to comfort the father. They wonder when they will see this son again. Even the tree looks a bit scattered and barren with grief.

We can think about this scene in many ways. Each of us may relate to it differently. Is it about greed and selfishness on the part of the son? Is it about the sadness and sense of loss when a child leaves his parents? Is it about leaving God— striking out on one's own and ignoring a sense of Holiness that has nourished us?

29. The Prodigal Turns

Luke 15:13b-19

✦ ✦ ✦ **A**nd there he squandered his property in dissolute living. When he had spent everything, a severe famine took place throughout that country, and he began to be in need. So he went and hired himself out to one of the citizens of that country, who sent him to his fields to feed the pigs. He would gladly have filled himself with the pods that the pigs were eating; and no one gave him anything.

But when he came to himself he said, 'How many of my father's hired hands have bread enough and to spare, but here I am dying of hunger! I will get up and go to my father, and I will say to him, "Father, I have sinned against heaven and before you; I am no longer worthy to be called your son; treat me like one of your hired hands."

The son wastes his inheritance in "dissolute living," and we can only imagine what that means. He loses everything and becomes so destitute that he is ready to eat the pods that feed the pigs!

Here is the moment when he "comes to himself." He wakes up with the realization that, in spite of his embarrassment, he must go home. Even his father's servants have food to eat. We wonder if he is remorseful and filled with love for his parents, or is he opportunistic and practical for his own very real needs?

If we consider the parable theologically and the parent represents God, then we might think about our own distance from God. What is life like without some kind of relationship with Holiness? Is it possible to return to a love larger than ourselves? Have you ever come to a realization such as this?

In this image, the son is still with the pig but I used the light and dark elements of the block to show him reaching out into the light. It is a wonderful moment of realization and turning. The pig seems to have his own sense of direction.

30. The Prodigal is Welcomed *Luke 15:20-21*

So he set off and went to his father. But while he was still far off, his father saw him and was filled with compassion; he ran and put his arms around him and kissed him. Then the son said to him, 'Father, I have sinned against heaven and before you; I am no longer worthy to be called your son.'

As a mother myself, I could not leave the mother out of this reunion when the wayward son returns. In spite of the son's great fear of what his parents will say, he must be surprised by the overwhelming welcome and forgiveness.

Again, people relate to this scene in a variety of ways. When have you been the one seeking forgiveness or in need of reconciliation? When have you been the one to offer forgiveness for one who has hurt you, whether it has been a family member or otherwise? Have you ever experienced a forgiving embrace of Infinite Love in the mystery of God?

31. The Celebration

Luke 15:22-24

But the father said to his slaves, 'Quickly, bring out a robe—the best one—and put it on him; put a ring on his finger and sandals on his feet. And get the fatted calf and kill it, and let us eat and celebrate; for this son of mine was dead and is alive again; he was lost and is found!' And they began to celebrate.

When the son returns, as in the other "lost and found" parables, there is the desire to celebrate with neighbors and friends. This joyful scene is not often portrayed in art. It is one of exorbitant hospitality and welcome. It is an outpouring of forgiveness and acceptance through a declaration to the neighborhood—without shame!

Perhaps it is all the more exuberant because the younger son erred so badly. In the story of the Woman with the Alabaster Jar, Jesus suggests that the greater the misdeed that is forgiven—the greater the expression of love. Although, from this younger son's point of view we are not told what he is thinking.

There are some details in the parable that you might see in the image: the signet ring, the best robe, the baskets of food, a woman with a tambourine, and the barren tree now shimmering in full leaf. If you look carefully, you can see the elder son coming over the hill from the field.

Forgiveness does not come easily for all members of the family. We might think about our own capabilities to sincerely forgive others, as well as our openness to receiving forgiveness from those we have harmed.

32. The Elder Brother *Luke 15:25-32*

"Now his elder son was in the field; and when he came and approached the house, he heard music and dancing. He called one of the slaves and asked what was going on. He replied, 'Your brother has come, and your father has killed the fatted calf, because he has got him back safe and sound.' Then he became angry and refused to go in. His father came out and began to plead with him.

But he answered his father, 'Listen! For all these years I have been working like a slave for you, and I have never disobeyed your command; yet you have never given me even a young goat so that I might celebrate with my friends. But when this son of yours came back, who has devoured your property with prostitutes, you killed the fatted calf for him!'

Then the father said to him, 'Son, you are always with me, and all that is mine is yours. But we had to celebrate and rejoice, because this brother of yours was dead and has come to life; he was lost and has been found.'"

In the last scene, the elder brother hears the music and celebration and comes from working in the field. When he learns that the brother who wasted the inheritance that should have gone to him has come home, he is furious. Here, he is clenching his hoe in jealousy and anger. He refuses to even look at his father who has come out to plead with him to join the celebration. This son asks why he has never received such a feast when he has obediently stayed home and worked for his father. The parable ends and it is left to our imagination whether the elder son finally turns to forgive his brother and join the party.

If we think of the ways we live out our faith, we might wonder about how we may obediently worship and do "good works" (as the elder son performed his duties), but not really yearn for connection with God.

This parable proclaims the power of abundant forgiveness and the hope that it offers for moving forward towards peace in many kinds of relationships. It seems that even in world politics, pride and jealousy interfere with resolutions of conflict. What would it mean for forgiveness and abundant compassion to be part of our political discourse?

33. As a Hen Gathers
Luke 13:31-34

At that very hour some Pharisees came and said to him, "Get away from here, for Herod wants to kill you." He said to them, "Go and tell that fox for me, 'Listen, I am casting out demons and performing cures today and tomorrow, and on the third day I finish my work. Yet today, tomorrow, and the next day I must be on my way, because it is impossible for a prophet to be killed outside of Jerusalem.'

Jerusalem, Jerusalem, the city that kills the prophets and stones those who are sent to it! How often have I desired to gather your children together as a hen gathers her brood under her wings, and you were not willing!..."

It is said that Jesus looked down from a hill above Jerusalem before he entered in his last days. He was filled with sadness over the oppression and injustice imposed on the people by Roman rule. In spite of the violence, Jesus tenderly expresses the desire to gather them all as a hen gathers her brood.

There is a beautiful chapel on this hill today called "the Church of Dominus Flevit" (where Jesus wept). The dome of the church is shaped like a tear drop. I believe Jesus longed for the people to come together peacefully within the love of an inclusive God. And yet they were not willing.

I stood on that hill outside of Jerusalem a few years ago and thought about the conflict there today. There is such fear on all sides: Israelis, of Palestinian uprising; and Palestinians, of the ongoing oppression and destruction of their homes and livelihood. Jesus, a Palestinian Jew himself, would weep even today. And yet there are those on both sides who long for and are working towards peace. They need our support.

In this image, I created two little chicks on separate blocks—these are the ones who are not willing to listen to the plea for compassion and forgiveness. They run away as fast as they can. Jesus demonstrated a larger wisdom of inclusive love that would bring people together—while also celebrating their differences.

34. Palm Sunday: Even the Stones

Luke 19:28-40

After he had said this, he went on ahead, going up to Jerusalem. When he had come near Bethphage and Bethany, at the place called the Mount of Olives, he sent two of the disciples, saying, "Go into the village ahead of you, and as you enter it you will find tied there a colt that has never been ridden. Untie it and bring it here. If anyone asks you, 'Why are you untying it?' just say this, 'The Lord needs it.'"

So those who were sent departed and found it as he had told them. As they were untying the colt, its owners asked them, "Why are you untying the colt?" They said, "The Lord needs it." Then they brought it to Jesus; and after throwing their cloaks on the colt, they set Jesus on it. As he rode along, people kept spreading their cloaks on the road. As he was now approaching the path down from the Mount of Olives, the whole multitude of the disciples began to praise God joyfully with a loud voice for all the deeds of power that they had seen, saying,

"Blessed is the king who comes in the name of the Lord!

Peace in heaven, and glory in the highest heaven!"

Some of the Pharisees in the crowd said to him, "Teacher, order your disciples to stop." He answered, "I tell you, if these were silent, the stones would shout out."

Palm Sunday offers a complex scene. If you look carefully, you can see the laying down of the cloaks in honor of Jesus riding in on a small colt or donkey, the waving of palms— even the Pharisee warning Jesus not to come into Jerusalem for fear of trouble. You may also see the Roman governor, Pontius Pilate, who is coming from another direction with his soldiers in tow to keep order. There is a rooster who reminds us of Peter's upcoming betrayal and perhaps warns us all of our doubts in the power of a way of nonviolent resistance.

I printed the block a second time, upside down over the image (after all, Jesus tries to turn our world around). Now the stones seem to sing out as Jesus said they would, even if his followers were told to be silent.

This is a story of rejoicing and praise. It is also a story of trepidation and fear knowing that there are forces that will not allow Jesus to continue teaching and healing through the love of an Infinite and All-Inclusive God.

35. Maundy Thursday Foot-Washing

John 13:1-17

Now before the festival of the Passover, Jesus knew that his hour had come to depart from this world and go to the Father. Having loved his own who were in the world, he loved them to the end. The devil had already put it into the heart of Judas son of Simon Iscariot to betray him. And during supper Jesus, knowing that the Father had given all things into his hands, and that he had come from God and was going to God, got up from the table, took off his outer robe, and tied a towel around himself. Then he poured water into a basin and began to wash the disciples' feet and to wipe them with the towel that was tied around him.

He came to Simon Peter, who said to him, "Lord, are you going to wash my feet?" Jesus answered, "You do not know now what I am doing, but later you will understand." Peter said to him, "You will never wash my feet." Jesus answered, "Unless I wash you, you have no share with me." Simon Peter said to him, "Lord, not my feet only but also my hands and my head!" Jesus said to him, "One who has bathed does not need to wash, except for the feet, but is entirely clean. And you are clean, though not all of you." For he knew who was to betray him; for this reason he said, "Not all of you are clean."

After he had washed their feet, had put on his robe, and had returned to the table, he said to them, "Do you know what I have done to you? You call me Teacher and Lord—and you are right, for that is what I am. So if I, your Lord and Teacher, have washed your feet, you also ought to wash one another's feet. For I have set you an example, that you also should do as I have done to you. Very truly, I tell you, servants are not greater than their master, nor are messengers greater than the one who sent them. If you know these things, you are blessed if you do them.

†

In this account from the book of John, it was the night before the Passover meal where Jesus had supper with the disciples. This is the only Gospel version that includes a foot-washing.

Jesus sets an example of humility, of forgetting ourselves in serving one another. But Simon Peter is so closed-up that, in the image, his toes are curled under as he tries to refuse to let Jesus wash his feet. He asks why Jesus doesn't wash his hands and head as well. Jesus says that if one has bathed, only his feet need washing. (Remember the dusty roads they surely walked each day.)

Jesus says that he is setting an example for them of serving others in this intimate and humble way. He breaks down the divisions of servant and master by recognizing equitable relationships of care and compassion.

This story of Peter's refusal, make me wonder how often I resist opportunities to make myself vulnerable to others in ways of serving and/or receiving blessing. After all, Jesus looks pretty excited to wash our feet!

36. Communion/Eucharist   *Mark 14:22-25*

While they were eating, he took a loaf of bread, and after blessing it he broke it, gave it to them, and said, "Take; this is my body." Then he took a cup, and after giving thanks he gave it to them, and all of them drank from it. He said to them, "This is my blood of the covenant, which is poured out for many. Truly I tell you, I will never again drink of the fruit of the vine until that day when I drink it new in the kingdom of God."

Communion (also called Eucharist, which means "thanksgiving") is a Christian ritual that has its roots in the stories of Jesus. He shared bread and wine with his disciples before his crucifixion, asking that they remember him— asking that they take into their very being, the story of his life and what he asks of them.

And in Communion, we might remember the great commandments that Jesus described as loving God with our whole selves, and loving our neighbors as ourselves. We might remember the forgiveness that Jesus demonstrated through the love of an infinite God. We might remember that we, too, are to live in this way—advocating for the poor and the oppressed.

People receive the Eucharist from a variety of traditions and it is a different experience for each person. It is one of our Christian rituals that is filled with mystery and beauty if we approach it with an openness that allows for new ways of seeing and being in the world. It is a tangible reminder that reinforces our commitment to the work of peace in our world.

The minister of a church which I attend, brings the two pieces of broken bread back together as she says the words, "Jesus said to 're-member' him." It is a visual reminder that by taking this way of making peace into our lives and actions, it is possible to bring back together wholeness where there is conflict and division. It is a life-long challenge.

In my image, I can imagine this broken bread being brought back together—surrounded by an incredible spirit of love.

37. When they Crucified Jesus...

John 19:23-31a, 38-42

When the soldiers had crucified Jesus, they took his clothes and divided them into four parts, one for each soldier. They also took his tunic; now the tunic was seamless, woven in one piece from the top. So they said to one another, "Let us not tear it, but cast lots for it to see who will get it." This was to fulfill what the scripture says, "They divided my clothes among themselves, and for my clothing they cast lots." And that is what the soldiers did.

Meanwhile, standing near the cross of Jesus were his mother, and his mother's sister, Mary the wife of Clopas, and Mary Magdalene.

When Jesus saw his mother and the disciple whom he loved standing beside her, he said to his mother, "Woman, here is your son." Then he said to the disciple, "Here is your mother." And from that hour the disciple took her into his own home.

After this, when Jesus knew that all was now finished, he said (in order to fulfill the scripture), "I am thirsty." A jar full of sour wine was standing there. So they put a sponge full of the wine on a branch of hyssop and held it to his mouth. When Jesus had received the wine, he said, "It is finished." Then he bowed his head and gave up his spirit.

Since it was the day of Preparation, the Jews did not want the bodies left on the cross during the Sabbath, especially because that Sabbath was a day of great solemnity....After these things, [one of the soldiers had pierced the side of Jesus with a spear] Joseph of Arimathea, who was a disciple of Jesus...asked Pilate to let him take away the body of Jesus. Pilate gave him permission; so he came and removed his body. Nicodemus, who had at first come to Jesus by night, also came, bringing a mixture of myrrh and aloes, weighing about a hundred pounds. They took the body of Jesus and wrapped it with the spices in linen cloths, according to the burial custom.... Now there was a garden in the place where he was crucified, and in the garden there was a new tomb in which no one had ever been laid. And so, because it was the Jewish day of Preparation, and the tomb was nearby, they laid Jesus there.

How could I possibly create an image of Jesus on the cross? I avoided facing this most poignant and painful scene in the Christian story. Finally, I drew the crucifixion from above and behind.

From this vantage point, we do see all that is going on below the cross as recorded in John—the soldiers bartering for the tunic, Mary kneeling in sorrow with another Mary beside her, the disciple (John) holding Mary's hand,

and Mary Magdalene reaching up in grief. Another soldier holds a spear, and branches of hyssop lie by the wayside. Further on this winding path from Jerusalem, Joseph of Arimathea and Nicodemus discuss bringing the body of Jesus to the tomb in the garden.

After cutting the block, I realized that everyone is the same size. Perhaps in God's eyes, there is incredible love for each one of us in spite of our "rightness or wrongness." It is not so much who was good and who was bad; even the soldiers probably thought they were doing the right thing under orders. Perhaps we are to find ourselves along this winding path from grief and guilt to resurrection and reconciliation.

I believe that Jesus died because he would not compromise who he was. He would not back down from his solidarity with those who had no voice—those who experienced sickness, and poverty, or were prejudiced against for whatever reason. He would not cooperate with the governing bodies who were wealthy at the expense of the poor. He saw the possibilities for good and God's infinite blessings, even in those who were seen as wrongdoers.

In the face of this painful death, Jesus did not call on armies to protect him; he never advocated violence in response to violence—and so, in his self-giving love, he was killed.

However, this is not the end of the story.

38. Easter Morning

Luke 24:1-9

But on the first day of the week, at early dawn, they came to the tomb, taking the spices that they had prepared. They found the stone rolled away from the tomb, but when they went in, they did not find the body. While they were perplexed about this, suddenly two men in dazzling clothes stood beside them. The women were terrified and bowed their faces to the ground, but the men said to them, "Why do you look for the living among the dead? He is not here, but has risen. Remember how he told you, while he was still in Galilee, that the Son of Man must be handed over to sinners, and be crucified, and on the third day rise again." Then they remembered his words, and returning from the tomb, they told all this to the eleven and to all the rest.

Hallelujah! This hard-to-believe story is the exuberance of faith—it is the ex-clamation mark! It is a story that puzzles many and inspires others. Is it the promise of life after death in a dimension we cannot understand as of yet? Is it a metaphor for the hope and the light that keeps us going even when things seem like they cannot get any worse? Is it the powerful notion that we need not be afraid; that in the love of an unimaginable and unending God, we can keep on living a life of faith, seeking peace and justice in our world?

It is in remembering Jesus and all those who have died in efforts of peace-making and speaking truth to power, that we are given strength to act in our own communities and world. We need not let fear hold us back.

The Infinite God of Peace—rises, still and always, in this great continuum of life!

39. On the Road to Emmaus *Luke 24:13-35*

Now on that same day two of them were going to a village called Emmaus, about seven miles from Jerusalem, and talking with each other about all these things that had happened. While they were talking and discussing, Jesus himself came near and went with them, but their eyes were kept from recognizing him. And he said to them, "What are you discussing with each other while you walk along?" They stood still, looking sad. Then one of them, whose name was Cleopas, answered him, "Are you the only stranger in Jerusalem who does not know the things that have taken place there in these days?"

He asked them, "What things?" They replied, "The things about Jesus of Nazareth, who was a prophet mighty in deed and word before God and all the people, and how our chief priests and leaders handed him over to be condemned to death and crucified him. But we had hoped that he was the one to redeem Israel. Yes, and besides all this, it is now the third day since these things took place.

Moreover, some women of our group astounded us. They were at the tomb early this morning, and when they did not find his body there, they came back and told us that they had indeed seen a vision of angels who said that he was alive. Some of those who were with us went to the tomb and found it just as the women had said; but they did not see him."

Then he said to them, "Oh, how foolish you are, and how slow of heart to believe all that the prophets have declared! Was it not necessary that the Messiah should suffer these things and then enter into his glory?" Then beginning with Moses and all the prophets, he interpreted to them the things about himself in all the scriptures.

As they came near the village to which they were going, he walked ahead as if he were going on. But they urged him strongly, saying, "Stay with us, because it is almost evening and the day is now nearly over." So he went in to stay with them. When he was at the table with them, he took bread, blessed and broke it, and gave it to them. Then their eyes were opened, and they recognized him; and he vanished from their sight.

They said to each other, "Were not our hearts burning within us while he was talking to us on the road, while he was opening the scriptures to us?" That same hour they got up and returned to Jerusalem; and they found the eleven and their companions gathered together. They were saying, "The Lord has risen indeed, and he has appeared to Simon!" Then they told what had happened on the road, and how he had been made known to them in the breaking of the bread.

Jesus appears incognito in this beautiful post-Easter story. Two of the followers of Jesus were walking along the Emmaus Road. One was named Cleopas and since the other one was not named, I like to imagine that it was his wife. They do not recognize Jesus and he asks them what they are talking about. They proceed to tell him about their hopes for one called Jesus, a prophet who did amazing works in the name of God. They tell him about the horrible crucifixion and the unbelievable story that angels were seen by women on that very day, saying that Jesus was still alive! This stranger on the road asks if they did not believe their prophets who foretold such things?

As they approach their village, the two ask him to come into their house as it is getting late. Around the table, the beautiful ritual of Communion is played out again as Jesus takes the bread, blesses it and breaks it to share with them. Incredibly, it was then that their "eyes were opened" and they recognize Jesus—just before he disappears.

It is a story filled with mystery and beauty. How would it be to hold open the notion that the Spirit of God's Love dwells in all human beings—and walks among us even now.

40. Swords into Plowshares   *Isaiah 2:2-4*

In days to come the mountain of the LORD'S house shall be established as the highest of the mountains, and shall be raised above the hills; all the nations shall stream to it. Many peoples shall come and say, "Come, let us go up to the mountain of the LORD, to the house of the God of Jacob; that he may teach us his ways and that we may walk in his paths."

For out of Zion shall go forth instruction, and the word of the LORD from Jerusalem.

He shall judge between the nations, and shall arbitrate for many peoples; they shall beat their swords into plowshares, and their spears into pruning hooks; nation shall not lift up sword against nation, neither shall they learn war any more.

†

Jesus must have loved this passage from his Hebrew scriptures. Perhaps it was one of the texts that made him so sad in the face of continued violence. Jesus was a peacemaker who showed us all how God's realm of fairness, peace and justice across all boundaries was possible then—and even now. In God's vision, this realm of peace could be attained without the use of violence and military force.

Where do you see this kind of non-violent striving for justice and peace in our times? I see it at work in so many peacemakers of our day like Sister Simone Campbell, who led nuns on a bus across the country to talk about our national budget and how unfair it is for those in poverty. I see it in the Combatants for Peace, who are both Israelis and Palestinians who put down weapons to work together for peace. I see it in the many climate change activists who understand that what happens to our earth not only affects our environment, but also has negative consequences for those around the world, many of whom already live in poverty.

Who do you support who is working nonviolently for peace? Who gives you hope in these days? I have to ask myself how my relationship with God, and this understanding of Jesus as peacemaker, leads me to work for peace in small ways and large ways. It is a challenge that is also—life-giving!

Notes

Acknowledgments

So many people have inspired me in faith, the arts, and in seeking peace for our world. First, I thank Paul Cohen and Colin Rolfe of Epigraph Publishing Service of Rhinebeck, NY, including copy-editor, Dory Mayo, who graciously made this book a reality. I thank the Rev. Heather Moody at the First Congregational United Church of Christ (UCC) in Poughkeepsie NY, the Rev. Dele, Rabbi Andrea Cohen-Kiener, Jo Anne Beemon, and Jay McDaniel for their passion for eco-theology and creation care. I thank the wonderful congregation at the Charlemont Federated Church in Massachusetts, where I was minister for ten years, especially for allowing me a sabbatical when some of these images were created. I thank the United Theological Seminary of the Twin Cities where Wilson Yates, Jann Cather Weaver, Cindi Beth Johnson, Eleazar Fernandez, and others taught me the importance of intersecting art, theology, and justice. So many clergy (Don Baker, Phil Schairbaum, Nancy and John Rohde, Tim Johnston, Jim Gertmenian, Kate Stevens, Mick Comstock, Dan Dibble, Marguerite Sheehan, Barbara Turner-Delisle, James Koyama, Rich Fournier, and Bert Marshall) as well as people in their congregations, have shown me how scripture is relevant to such issues as racism, poverty, women's equality, our environment, and peace.

I am grateful to my (late) parents, Vernon and Mary Reed Bobbitt. As an art professor at Albion College, my father inspired me with his eclectic creativity and his ability to see beauty in all things. My mother inspired me with her literary interests, her humor, and her deep faith. She taught me how to pray—and both my parents helped me to see beauty as reflections of the Divine. I thank my sister, Sue Haas, for her love of the arts and her enthusiasm for my many projects. I thank my husband, Jeffrey, for his artistic eye, quiet strength, and loving support. I thank our dear daughter, Anna, for her encouragement, her helpful critique, and her own work in environmentally sustainable landscapes. So many others have inspired me in living and loving, faith-building and peacemaking—I am truly grateful.

About the Author

The Rev. Cara B. Hochhalter is a retired United Church of Christ (UCC) minister. She received her Masters of Divinity from United Theological Seminary of the Twin Cities in Minnesota, where she studied the intersections of art, theology, and justice. She says, "I find that the process of creating images becomes a means to break into Biblical texts and themes that are meaningful in today's world." Cara is an artist, a teacher, a peacemaker, and has served as minister for a church in Charlemont, Massachusetts for ten years. She now resides in Hyde Park, New York with her husband, Jeffrey. She enjoys gardening with native plants, making watercolor/graphite art of wildflowers, and participating in peace efforts. Cara and Jeffrey have one daughter, Anna, who is a landscape architect with an ecological focus.

CPSIA information can be obtained
at www.ICGtesting.com
Printed in the USA
BVHW031922110222
628797BV00005B/221